T0040293

the HARD SELTZER

cocktail book

the HARD SELTZER

cocktail book

55 (UNOFFICIAL) Recipes
for White Claw® Slushies,
Truly® Mixers, *and More*
Spiked-Seltzer Drinks

Casie Vogel

ULYSSES PRESS

Published in the US by:
Ulysses Press
PO Box 3440
Berkeley, CA 94703
www.ulyssespress.com

ISBN: 978-1-64604-185-5
Library of Congress Control Number: 2021930799

Printed in China
10 9 8 7 6 5 4 3 2 1

Managing editor: Claire Chun
Editor: Anne Healey
Proofreader: Renee Rutledge
Front cover design: David Hastings
Cover artwork: blue background © Magenta10/shutterstock.com; drinks
    © VECTOR FUN/shutterstock.com
Interior artwork: shutterstock.com except pages 29, 55, 79, 83, 91, 111
    © Michael Calcagno

To Michael

Contents

CHAPTER THREE: CLASSY CLASSICS 81

CHAPTER FOUR: PREGAME & PARTY 115

Introduction

Nothing sounds sweeter than the crack of that slim aluminum can, home to a 100-calorie bubbly beauty. Spring, summer, whatever the time of year, it's hard seltzer season.

At 4 to 6 percent alcohol content, it's not a bad deal! But sometimes you have to take it up a notch...or several. I mean, that's what we're all here for if we're being honest, right? Hard seltzer (also called spiked seltzer) is the perfect mixer to make a boozy drink that much boozier.

What's the right ratio? What actually tastes like a cocktail, doesn't skimp, but also doesn't immediately send you to blackout town? Well, my friend, that is where my help comes in. The recipes from here on out are dangerously delicious and designed to get the party going, whether it's a Friday night pregame or your next big party—or if it's just been a tough day (girl, you do you). Instead of that next round of probably (always) regrettable tequila shots, pick up this book and let's get bubbly.

WHAT IS HARD SELTZER, ANYWAY?

You may have noticed in stores that hard seltzer is in the refrigerated display case with all the beer. But it's not exactly beer, is it? The production process is very similar to beer, but seltzer is made from fermented cane sugar instead of malted barley. Most seltzers are advertised as being made with "real fruit juice," which is true (at least for the major brands)! That's where the flavor comes from—not from artificial sweeteners. As a result, we get to enjoy drinks that are low in calories and low in sugar. As an added bonus, most seltzers are gluten-free as well!

TYPES OF HARD SELTZER

As of this writing, there are a ton of different seltzer brands. Wherever you're reading this from, you have no doubt encountered the major players, such as White Claw, Truly, and Spiked Seltzer; but there are also tons of local booze players trying to get into this game. My scientific research[1] has shown that for the most part the seltzer flavors listed here often overlap between brands. In this book I've tried to use an assortment of the readily available flavors, so you should be able to find them at most stores. If you're having trouble, you can and should definitely trust your taste buds in terms of substitutions. Here's my advice on improvising with the various seltzer flavors:

Citrus flavors. When it comes to the "classics," citrus flavors—like lemon, orange, tangerine, clementine, grapefruit, and lime—are a must-have and are the easiest to swap out. Lime is by far the strongest of the citrus flavors; I personally feel it has a little more kick. When replacing, make sure to taste test.

---

1 Just kidding; do not mistake the author for someone who has any knowledge of science.

Berry flavors. Berry flavors include strawberry, raspberry, cranberry, and mixed berry; they are pretty strong, so I wouldn't recommend mixing them with a dark liquor. They are great for upgrading your basic drinks without adding flavored syrup. For example, upgrading a classic lime daiquiri to raspberry would just require swapping out lime (or any other flavor) seltzer for raspberry seltzer!

Black cherry. You're either a black cherry person or you're not. If you are, you're in luck because the superstrong flavor profile will overpower most drinks. If you're looking to mask a ton of liquor, even tequila, black cherry is your new BFF. I don't include black cherry as a suggestion in many of these recipes because it is so overpowering. But if you really love it, feel free to swap it in.

"Tropical" flavors. Choices like passionfruit, pineapple, mango, and strawberry kiwi really shine in the frozen/slushy drinks, but feel free to mix and match.

Seasonal flavors. As of this writing, many of the major brands have come out with "seasonal" flavors that may or may not be available depending on when you're making these drinks. For example, in fall 2020, Bud Light debuted the Ugly Sweater variety pack, which included fall/winter-themed flavors like Apple Crisp and Ginger Snap. For the seasonal drinks, I've noted where you could give such seltzers a try. I've only suggested seasonal flavors for the holiday drinks and have offered substitutions if you don't have them on hand.

Sparkling hard cider. Many cideries are also making hard seltzer, or "sparkling" cider. Those are more apple-flavored than many of the traditional spiked seltzer flavors, but they work great in sangrias and tropical drinks. While sparkling cider is not technically a hard seltzer, I'm open to the substitution if you have it on hand!

Hard lemonade. Some of our go-to brands, such as Truly, have lemonade flavors that are particularly nice in the frozen cocktails. But brands like Mike's Hard Lemonade have been around forever and are essentially the same thing. You can absolutely use those as well!

> Trust your taste buds and use the flavors that you like. If you don't like pineapple, swap it out for another flavor. If you're not sure how to choose a substitution, just use a flavor you do like from the same variety pack. The other flavors that come in the box are often good choices.

OTHER BOOZE TO HAVE ON HAND

The recipes in this book range from classic martinis to jungle juice. If you want to make them all, you may need to start stocking your bar. Classic liquors are always good to have around, but make sure to check recipes for some of the more out-there punches, which use some less common liquors and liqueurs!

THE CLASSICS

While there are plenty more liquors out there that you can have on your bar cart, the necessary ones for this book are listed below. Believe it or not, it's not just clear liquors on this list!

- ✦ Bourbon
- ✦ Brandy
- ✦ Cognac
- ✦ Cointreau or triple sec
- ✦ Gin
- ✦ Rum (dark and light)
- ✦ Rye
- ✦ Tequila (the blanco, or silver, variety)
- ✦ Vermouth (dry and sweet varieties)
- ✦ Vodka

WINE

I hope that this is obvious, but don't go using that bottle of wine you've been saving since your trip to Paris for the recipes in this book. Use wines that you like, but certainly don't spend more than $20 on a bottle. Here are some suggested wines to have around:

- ✦ Prosecco or other sparkling white wine
- ✦ Red wine, ideally Spanish for sangria
- ✦ Rosé
- ✦ White wine

LESS COMMON LIQUEURS

You don't need to go crazy here, but you may need some less common liqueurs to round out these drinks. It's always smart to have a bottle (or two) of Aperol at the ready—every party loves a spritz!

- Aperol (a bitter, bright orange Italian apéritif)
- Blue curaçao (a bright blue liqueur from Curaçao that's flavored with laraha, a native bitter orange)
- Campari (a bitter, dark red Italian apéritif)
- Coconut-flavored rum (such as Malibu)
- Peach schnapps

MIXERS, GARNISHES, AND OTHER ACCOUTREMENTS

It's not just about the booze! You'll need some nonalcoholic additions to make your cocktails complete. This list has everything, from your classic mixers (like orange juice and cranberry juice cocktail) to the unexpected (like soy sauce and vanilla ice cream).

MIXERS

There's a lot of juice on this list of mixers. If you can find it (or squeeze it), fresh juice is always preferable.

the **HARD SELTZER** *cocktail book*

- Apple cider or juice
- Bitters (such as Angostura or Peychaud's)
- Black tea
- Cola soft drink
- Cranberry juice cocktail
- Cream of coconut
- Fruit punch
- Ginger beer
- Grapefruit juice
- Grenadine
- Lemon juice
- Lemonade
- Lime juice
- Orange juice
- Peach or apricot puree/nectar
- Pineapple juice
- Simple syrup
- Soda water
- Tomato juice or Clamato

Easy Simple Syrup

There's no reason to buy simple syrup—it's supereasy to make it yourself. I like to have some available at all times. You never know when you want a cocktail ASAP! Make some now and keep it handy.

The ratio is 1:1; you can scale this up or down as needed. Store the syrup in the fridge, and it should keep for about four weeks.

> 1 cup white sugar
> 1 cup water

1. Combine the sugar and water in a small saucepan over medium heat.

2. Stir until the sugar is dissolved. Remove from the heat and let cool completely.

3. Pour the syrup into an airtight glass container (I like to use a mason jar), and store it in the fridge.

OTHER ITEMS USED IN THESE RECIPES

You can keep these around for non-booze-related activities, too. Odds are you have most of them in your pantry or fridge already!

- Hot sauce
- Jell-O/gelatin
- Milk
- Soy sauce
- Vanilla extract
- Vanilla or raspberry ice cream
- Worcestershire sauce

FRESH/FROZEN FRUITS AND VEGETABLES

Frozen fruit is great for frozen drinks because it cuts down on how much ice you need to have on hand. If you don't like a particular fruit or are allergic, just swap it out for another you prefer instead.

- Cranberries, fresh
- Cucumber
- Grapefruit
- Green apple
- Lemon
- Lime
- Mango chunks, frozen
- Mixed berries, frozen and fresh
- Orange
- Seedless watermelon, fresh
- Strawberries, frozen and fresh

the **HARD SELTZER** *cocktail book*

GARNISHES

Are garnishes absolutely necessary? No. Are they classy AF? You bet. Adding a fresh rosemary sprig or cinnamon stick to your cocktail can be the perfect touch for your Instagram story.

- Celery
- Celery salt
- Chili powder
- Cinnamon
- Egg whites
- Maraschino cherries
- Mint, fresh
- Nutmeg, ground

- Olives
- Paprika
- Pepper
- Rosemary, fresh
- Sea salt
- Sugar
- Sugar cubes

TOOLS YOU'LL NEED

You don't need to buy a fancy bartender's kit for these recipes, but you will need a few crucial supplies. If you're packing items for a bachelorette weekend or just want to make sure your kitchen is outfitted, here are the essentials:

Bar spoon. This is really just a long spoon for mixing cocktails that aren't shaken. If you don't have a bar spoon, you can substitute with the longest spoon in your kitchen.

Blender. Any stationary blender will work for frozen cocktails.

Cocktail shaker. Also known as a "cobbler shaker," the classic cocktail shaker consists of a cup, strainer, and lid, perfect for shaking, mixing, and pouring.

Ice pop molds and wooden sticks. These are only used for the Clawsicles (page 65). Not all ice pop molds require wooden sticks, so check what kind of molds you have.

Juicer. I highly recommend using fresh juice whenever you can. A small manual juicer is great to have; mine fits on top of a mason jar and doesn't take up too much room in my drawers.

Large pitcher or punch bowl. Select a pitcher or punch bowl that can hold at least a gallon; you'll want to make sure that you have enough to go around for the party drinks.

Measuring cups. When it comes to large-batch cocktails, you'll put away the shot glass and start working with larger quantities, so you will need measuring cups in three sizes: ¼ cup, ½ cup, and 1 cup.

Paring knife and small cutting board. A small knife and cutting board will be nice to have for slicing lime wedges and other garnishes.

Plastic condiment cups. These are only used for the Sparkling Jell-O Shots (page 120). Usually 2 ounces, these often come with plastic lids that are great for storing in the fridge.

Shot glass. A shot glass is a must-have. Most are 1 or 2 ounces; make sure you know what size you have so you don't under- or over-pour. This is used for measuring, so if you're buying a new

the HARD SELTZER cocktail book

shot glass, I recommend getting one with fill lines that show the amounts on the side.

SELTZER-FRIENDLY GLASSWARE

I've offered suggestions for glassware where appropriate, but honestly, these are some pretty hefty cocktails. Unfortunately, all those cute coupes and dainty champagne glasses are out of the picture unless you're serving from a pitcher. I've downsized this glassware list to the major oversized glassware (and some more creative variations) that can hold anywhere from 8 to 16 ounces of liquid. Feel free to pick and choose when you're crafting these recipes!

Oversized cocktail glasses. You probably know the cocktail glass as a martini glass. Most martini glasses that you buy at the store these days are technically "oversized"; make sure yours are properly huge (more than 10-ounce capacity).

Double old-fashioned glasses. Also known as a rocks glass. Make sure you've got doubles—these cocktails are certainly not singles.

Wine glasses. Don't try to break out those tiny free glasses you got at a wine tasting; you are going to need the big mamas for these cocktails. I recommend using white-wine glasses over red because they're designed to keep drinks cooler for longer.

Margarita glasses. These shallow-bowled, wide-rimmed glasses aren't just for margs! Feel free to break these out for any of the frozen cocktails.

Hurricane glasses. Nothing screams "hot summer days" like the curves of a hurricane glass.

Copper mugs. This one is traditionally used to serve a Moscow mule, but it's great for these cocktails if you want to keep things cool and classy.

Pint glasses. Your classic beer glass is perfect for these cocktails. It's got the capacity to handle ice, seltzer, and liquor.

Highball glasses. Tall and skinny, these glasses work well for all types of cocktails and are sure to impress in a pinch. A Collins glass is similar and works well also; the only difference is that it's slightly taller.

Mason jars. Not a traditional cocktail glass by any means, but it's a great (and cheap) way to keep it classy, serve a crowd, and still contain all that fizzy goodness.

Solo cups. I had to add it. Your trusty red plastic Solo cup absolutely does the trick here. It's certainly less classy, but no one said that you couldn't have a martini in a red cup.

A NOTE ON RECIPES AND ORGANIZATION

The recipes are organized into four different chapters based on the potential party you're hosting or the day-drinking situation you've found yourself in. For example, Chapter One, "Boozy Brunch," is full of your late-morning favorites, from mimosas to micheladas. If you're looking for a specific drink, you can always flip to the index.

With the exception of a few single-serving cocktails and the batch "party" cocktails, most of the recipes in this book use one 12-ounce can of hard seltzer and serve two. Feel free to scale up or down as needed.

Boozy Brunch

All hail, the queen of all meals: brunch.

No one is immune to her charms. I mean, who doesn't love brunch? Whether it's a bottomless deal or just the promise of day drinking with friends, a bubbly drink with your first meal of the day is the perfect weekend treat.

And hard seltzer is a crowning addition to a brunch cocktail. It pairs perfectly with icons like the Aperol spritz, Bellini, and mimosa and adds an interesting twist to savory girls like the Bloody Mary.

Whether you're enjoying brunch at home with the girls or looking to keep brunch vibes going well after your two-hour limit is up, this chapter has you covered.

Mega Mimosa

The brunch classic...but with a lot more booze. I like my mimosa to be light on the orange juice—with just enough to provide a bit of color. Add or subtract orange juice depending on how you like yours.

MAKES 2 DRINKS

6 ounces prosecco or sparkling white wine

1 (12-ounce) can orange hard seltzer

orange juice, to taste

✦ Split the prosecco and the seltzer between two glasses.

✦ Top with the orange juice to taste.

> Any citrus-flavor hard seltzer will work great here! I highly recommend trying it out with grapefruit, pineapple, or mango. This recipe can also be doubled, tripled, or quadrupled depending on the size of your brunch party.

Boozier Bellini

Bellinis aren't typically served over ice, but since these are rather large drinks, I recommend throwing in a few cubes to keep things cool as you sip. Orange or tangerine hard seltzer is a good alternative here if you don't have mango on hand.

MAKES 2 DRINKS

4 ounces peach or apricot puree/nectar

6 ounces prosecco or other sparkling white wine

1 (12-ounce) can mango hard seltzer

peach slices, for garnish

✦ Fill two glasses with ice. Split the peach or apricot puree between the glasses.

✦ Top each glass with 3 ounces of prosecco followed by half a can (6 ounces) of seltzer.

✦ Drop in the peach slices and serve.

Quadruple this recipe if you want to use an entire bottle of sparkling wine.

Aperol Spritz-o-Clock

This classic Italian apéritif isn't just good before a meal—it's always spritz-o-clock in my book. You can use soda water instead of the prosecco, but it's much more fun to triple down on the alcohol.

MAKES 2 DRINKS

6 ounces Aperol

4 ounces prosecco or soda water

1 (12-ounce) can orange hard seltzer

orange wedges, for garnish

✦ Fill two glasses with ice. Split the Aperol between the glasses (3 ounces each).

✦ Split the prosecco or soda water between the glasses (2 ounces each).

✦ Top each glass with half a can (6 ounces) of seltzer. Garnish each glass with an orange wedge.

Spritzy Screwdriver

The screwdriver is a dangerously delicious brunch choice; imbibe carefully. For this one, try out some different hard seltzer flavors, such as mango, pineapple, or grapefruit.

MAKES 2 DRINKS

3 ounces vodka

6 ounces orange juice

1 (12-ounce) can orange hard seltzer

orange wedges, for garnish

✦ Fill two glasses with ice. Add 1½ ounces of vodka to each glass.

✦ Split the orange juice between the two glasses (3 ounces each).

✦ Top each glass with half a can (6 ounces) of seltzer. Garnish each with an orange wedge.

Fizzy Fuzzy Navel

Make brunch totally rad with this classic '80s cocktail. This twist brings it into the 2020s by adding some bodacious bubbles.

MAKES 2 DRINKS

¼ cup peach schnapps

¼ cup orange juice

1 (12-ounce) can orange hard seltzer

orange wedges, for garnish

+ Fill a cocktail shaker with ice. Add the peach schnapps and the orange juice. Stir.

+ Strain into two glasses filled with ice.

+ Top each glass with half a can (6 ounces) of seltzer. Garnish each with an orange wedge.

> Try this one with pineapple or mango seltzer!

Lazy Gal's Greyhound

Grapefruit is my go-to hard seltzer flavor. I've been known to spike it more than once with a little vodka and make what I call a "Lazy Gal's Greyhound." It's definitely better with grapefruit juice, but I've marked it as optional in the event that you are just looking to keep it fast and loose.

MAKES 1 DRINK

1 ounce vodka

1 (12-ounce) can grapefruit hard seltzer

1–2 ounces grapefruit juice, to taste (optional)

✦ Fill a pint glass with ice and add all the ingredients. Stir gently (this will be a full glass!)

Bubbly Mary

Don't repeat this one too many times. Not that you'll summon Bloody Mary—but you may summon a hangover. I like lemon hard seltzer for this recipe, but feel free to try it with lime!

MAKES 1 DRINK

SALT RIM
1 teaspoon celery salt

1 teaspoon black pepper

1 teaspoon smoked paprika

✦ Combine the salt rim ingredients in a small bowl. Pour onto a small plate.

✦ Rub the lemon wedge around the rim of a glass to moisten it. Place the juiced rim on the plate with the salt rim mix, pressing gently to coat it. Fill the glass with ice.

BUBBLY MARY

1 lemon wedge

1 ounce vodka

3 ounces tomato juice or Clamato

1 dash Worcestershire sauce

2 dashes hot sauce (such as Tabasco)

1 tablespoon lime juice

1 tablespoon lemon juice

½ (12-ounce) can lemon hard seltzer (approximately 6 ounces)

celery, olives, cornichons, shrimp, and/or bacon, for garnish

✦ Fill a cocktail shaker with ice. Add all the ingredients except the garnishes.

✦ Shake a few times to combine. Don't overshake—you don't want to shake all the bubbles out of the seltzer.

✦ Strain into the prepared glass. Add any desired garnishes.

Más Michelada

Find your beach without the beer. Lime hard seltzer is the perfect substitute.

MAKES 1 DRINK

SPICE MIX
1 teaspoon
chili powder

½ teaspoon
coarse sea salt

MICHELADA
1 lime wedge

1 dash
Worcestershire sauce

1 dash soy sauce

1 dash hot sauce
(such as Tabasco)

1 ounce lime juice

3 ounces tomato
juice or Clamato

1 (12-ounce) can
lime hard seltzer

lime wheel, for
garnish (optional)

✦ Combine the chili powder and the sea salt in a small bowl. Spread onto a small plate.

✦ Rub the lime wedge around the rim of a glass to moisten it. Place the moistened rim onto the plate with the spice mix, pressing gently to coat it.

✦ Fill the glass with ice. Add a pinch of the spice mix to the glass.

✦ Add all the remaining ingredients except the garnish. Gently stir to mix. Garnish with the lime wedge or lime wheel.

One-Minute Margarita (On the Rocks)

Check out page 77 for a big-batch frozen margarita recipe, but if you're looking for a quick on-the-rocks version, you're in the right place.

MAKES 2 DRINKS

1 lime wedge, to rim glass (optional)

sea salt, to rim glass (optional)

3 ounces blanco tequila

1 ounce Cointreau

2 ounces lime juice

1 (12-ounce) can lime hard seltzer

lime wheels, for garnish

+ If a salt rim is desired, rub the lime wedge around the rims of two glasses to moisten. Dip the rims in the sea salt to coat.

+ Fill the glasses with ice.

+ Fill a cocktail shaker with ice. Add the tequila, Cointreau, lime juice, and seltzer. Shake until chilled.

+ Strain into the glasses. Garnish each with a lime wheel.

You can play around with seltzer flavors on this one. Strawberry and raspberry are great ways to make this go from the classic lime margarita to a flavored margarita without added fruit or syrup.

Tequila Sunrise to Sunset

Since brunch never happens at sunrise, this is a nice consolation prize. Of course, if you do this right, brunch might last until sunset!

MAKES 2 DRINKS

4 ounces blanco tequila

8 ounces orange juice

1 (12-ounce) can orange hard seltzer

2 teaspoons grenadine

maraschino cherries, for garnish

orange wheels, for garnish

✦ Fill two glasses with ice. Split the tequila, orange juice, and seltzer between them. Stir until mixed.

✦ Add 1 teaspoon of the grenadine to each glass, allowing it to sink to the bottom.

✦ Garnish each glass with a maraschino cherry and an orange wheel.

Although the recipe calls for orange seltzer, any of the tropical-flavor seltzers will work here! Pineapple is a nice spin. It's tempting to use black cherry seltzer in place of the grenadine here, but I feel it doesn't give the drink that same flavor. Plus, you don't get the red sunrise look without the grenadine.

Dealer's Choice White Sangria

In this recipe, hard seltzer stands in for the flavored liquor that's usually found in sangria. This is a true dealer's choice—pick any of your favorite hard seltzer flavors. I suggest grapefruit or strawberry! Feel free to mix up the fruit to match whatever seltzer you choose.

MAKES 4–6 DRINKS

1 (750-milliliter) bottle white wine, chilled

1 cup strawberries, halved

1 large orange, sliced

1 large green apple, cubed

2 ounces simple syrup (optional)

1–2 (12-ounce) cans hard seltzer (any flavor), to taste

✦ Combine all the ingredients in a pitcher. Serve over ice.

✦ If making ahead, combine all the ingredients except the seltzer, and store in the fridge. Just before serving, add the seltzer to the pitcher and stir, then pour into glasses. This maximizes bubbles!

Dealer's Choice
Red Sangria

Another dealer's choice when it comes to your choice of hard seltzer flavor. For red sangria, I suggest going with a citrus flavor, like lemon, lime, orange, or grapefruit.

**MAKES
4–6 DRINKS**

1 (750-milliliter) bottle red wine, ideally Spanish

1 large orange, sliced

1 lemon, sliced

1 large green apple, cubed

2 ounces simple syrup (optional)

1–2 (12-ounce) cans hard seltzer (any flavor), to taste

✦ Combine all the ingredients in a pitcher. Serve over ice.

✦ If making ahead, combine all the ingredients except the seltzer, and store in the fridge. Just before serving, add the seltzer to the pitcher and stir, then pour. This maximizes bubbles!

Mom's White Wine Spritzer

The wine spritzer isn't just for moms. True day drinkers know that this drink is actually the ultimate brunch power move. It's the best way to guarantee a buzz that lasts for hours. With this spiked seltzer combo, you'll have to admit, your mom was right about this one.

MAKES 1 DRINK

3 ounces white wine, chilled

½ (12-ounce) can lime hard seltzer, chilled (approximately 6 ounces)

lime wheel, for garnish

✦ Fill a large wine glass with ice (this is optional; if all the ingredients are very, very cold you can skip the ice).

✦ Add the wine. Top with the seltzer.

✦ Garnish with the lime wheel.

If you'd like to scale up or down, the ratio here is 1 part wine, 2 parts seltzer.

CHAPTER TWO

Summer Slushies

How to describe spiked seltzer on a hot summer day? Talented, brilliant, incredible, amazing, show-stopping, spectacular, never the same, completely not ever been done before, unafraid to reference or not reference, put it in a blender.[2]

Actually, blending hard seltzer into frozen cocktails has definitely been done before by many on social media. This chapter is packed with some classic frozen beverages, such as your margarita or daiquiri, but there are also some fun surprises, like the Boozy Berry Smoothie (page 57), inspired by the Costco food court, and Clawsicles (page 65). You heard me. Clawsicles.

Changing up flavors for any of these recipes is encouraged unless otherwise noted.

---

2 Attributed to Lady Gaga, aka Mother Monster. Not in reference to seltzer, but you get the idea.

Sparkling Frosé

A summertime stunner, frosé will steal the show at any poolside soiree. It requires some forethought, because you have to freeze the rosé the night before. That's the only way you can achieve that really perfect slushy texture. Trust me—it's worth it.

**MAKES
4-6 DRINKS**

1 (750-milliliter) bottle rosé wine

1 cup strawberries, frozen

1-2 ounces simple syrup, to taste

1 (12-ounce) can grapefruit hard seltzer

✦ Pour the wine into a gallon-size zip-lock bag. Freeze overnight.

✦ The next day add the strawberries, frozen rosé, and simple syrup to a blender. Blend until smooth.

✦ Add the seltzer and pulse a few times to mix.

✦ Serve immediately.

Watermelon Sugar Slushy

🍋 🍋 🍋

This watermelon slushy is dangerously refreshing—perfect for a hot day at the beach. Or for pretending that it's a hot day at the beach. In Malibu. With Harry Styles. Okay, too hot! Freeze the watermelon overnight; it is best served as cold as possible.

MAKES 4-6 DRINKS

4 cups seedless watermelon, chopped

1 cup vodka

2 ounces lime juice

1–2 ounces simple syrup, to taste

1 (12-ounce) can watermelon or lime hard seltzer

1 lime wedge, to rim glasses (optional)

sugar, to rim glasses (optional)

lime wheels, for garnish

✦ Put the watermelon in a large ziplock bag. Place in the freezer for a minimum of 1 hour, but ideally overnight.

✦ The next day, put the watermelon, vodka, lime juice, and simple syrup in a blender. Puree until the watermelon is completely liquefied.

✦ Add the seltzer and pulse a few times. You don't want to blend out all the bubbles, but you want this well mixed.

✦ If desired, rub a lime wedge around the rims of two large glasses. Dip in sugar.

✦ Pour into prepared glasses and garnish with lime wedges.

the **HARD SELTZER** *cocktail book*

Boozy Berry Smoothie

Inspired by Costco's iconic mixed berry smoothie (we are high class here), this boozy concoction is perfect for that bag of bulk frozen berries. Feel free to use any berry hard seltzer here.

MAKES 4–6 DRINKS

¼ cup vodka

3–4 cups frozen mixed berries

1–2 ounces simple syrup, to taste

1–2 (12-ounce) cans berry hard seltzer, to taste

✦ Add the vodka, berries, and simple syrup to a blender. Blend until smooth.

✦ Add the first can of seltzer. Pulse until combined. Depending on desired consistency, add the second can.

✦ Serve immediately.

NSFW Frozen Lemonade

This sparkling frozen lemonade is a great twist on the sidewalk stand classic. But you'd probably need to get a liquor license for a neighborhood stand...so this one is better saved for your own personal enjoyment.

MAKES 4–6 DRINKS

½ cup vodka

1 cup bottled lemonade

6–8 cups ice

1–2 (12-ounce) cans lemonade hard seltzer, to taste

1–3 ounces simple syrup, to taste (optional)

✦ Add the vodka, lemonade, and ice to a blender. Blend until smooth.

✦ Add the first can of seltzer. Pulse until combined. Depending on desired consistency, add the second can.

✦ For a sweeter lemonade, add the simple syrup to taste. Pulse.

✦ Serve immediately.

> If you don't have lemonade seltzer on hand, you can absolutely just use lemon seltzer or another lemonade-friendly flavor like strawberry or raspberry.

the **HARD SELTZER** cocktail book

No Sleep 'til Mango Slushy

Don't sleep on mango! Mango hard seltzer is perfect for blended cocktails. While you can add it to the frozen margarita (page 77) and frozen daiquiri (page 66) recipes for flavor, this vodka version is just as tasty.

MAKES 4–6 DRINKS

6 ounces vodka

2 ounces Cointreau

2 cups frozen mango chunks

1–2 ounces simple syrup, to taste

2–4 cups ice

1 (12-ounce) can mango hard seltzer

✦ Add all the ingredients to a blender. Blend.

✦ Serve immediately.

Adult Orange Julius

You're at your hometown mall. After loitering in the bookstore and the fast-fashion stores, you head to the food court. Where is your clique spending their allowance? The Orange Julius, obviously.

MAKES
4-6 DRINKS

½ cup orange juice

½ cup vodka

1 cup milk

1-2 ounces simple syrup, to taste

½ teaspoon vanilla extract

4-6 cups ice

1 (12-ounce) can orange hard seltzer

✦ Add all the ingredients to a blender. Blend. Serve immediately.

> If you are old enough to drink but too young to have encountered an Orange Julius, just kill me now.

Clawsicles

It's genius. The Claw meets Popsicles in this spiked seltzer pop, a perfect summertime treat. Feel free to change up the fruit and seltzer flavors (try pineapple or mango) for different variations.

MAKES 6 ICE POPS

1 cup mixed berries

1 ounce simple syrup (optional)

1 (12-ounce) can raspberry hard seltzer

✦ Blend the berries and the simple syrup, if using, into a puree.

✦ Spoon about a tablespoon of the puree into six ice pop molds.

✦ Fill the molds with the seltzer, being careful not to overfill. Add the pop sticks (either wooden or plastic, depending on what type of mold you have). Freeze overnight.

✦ Once the ice pops are frozen, run hot water over the molds to release. Enjoy immediately!

Of course, it's not necessary to use White Claw for these "Clawsicles." "Trusicles" or "Bud Light Seltzersicles" just didn't have the same ring to it. Feel free to use any brand here!

Sloshed Strawberry Daiquiri

Strawberry. Raspberry. Pineapple. Mango. Just swap out the strawberry seltzer for a different flavor without any added fruit or syrup. It's that easy!

MAKES
4–6 DRINKS

4 ounces white rum

2 ounces lime juice

4–6 cups ice

1–2 ounces simple syrup, to taste

1 (12-ounce) can strawberry hard seltzer

✦ Add all the ingredients except the seltzer to a blender. Blend until smooth.

✦ Add the seltzer and pulse a few times. Serve immediately.

> If you end up going with a different flavor, such as mango or pineapple, the flavor will be there, but the color won't. If you're trying to achieve an aesthetic, just add in a handful of whatever color frozen fruit pairs with the seltzer you're using.

Peak Heat Piña Colada

Everyone likes piña coladas. Getting caught in the rain? Not so much. Enjoy this on a hot summer day.

MAKES 4–6 DRINKS

½ cup light rum

¼ cup cream of coconut

2 ounces pineapple juice

1 (12-ounce) can pineapple hard seltzer

4–6 cups ice

✦ Add all the ingredients to a blender. Blend until smooth.

✦ Serve immediately.

No Drama
Bahama Mama

Maybe you've had quite the week. Or year. Set your sights on that upcoming vacation, and imagine yourself beachside with this cocktail in hand. You're the Bahama mama now.

**MAKES
4–6 DRINKS**

3 ounces dark rum

3 ounces coconut rum (such as Malibu)

3 ounces pineapple juice

1 orange, juiced

1 lime, juiced

splash of grenadine

4–6 cups ice

1 (12-ounce) can pineapple hard seltzer, to taste

✦ Add all the ingredients except the seltzer to a blender. Blend until smooth.

✦ Add the seltzer. Pulse until just combined.

✦ Serve immediately.

The 9-to-5 Pain Killer

Long day at work? Email headache? Nothing takes the edge off like a painkiller. Watch your pours, however. If you're too heavy-handed, I can't guarantee you won't have a different kind of headache tomorrow morning.

MAKES 4–6 DRINKS

¼ cup dark rum

¼ cup pineapple juice

2 ounces orange juice

2 ounces cream of coconut

4–6 cups ice

1 (12-ounce) can orange or pineapple hard seltzer

ground nutmeg, for garnish

+ Add all the ingredients to a blender. Blend until smooth.

+ Garnish with ground nutmeg. Serve immediately.

Fizztastic
Frozen Paloma

This tart slushy is a nice break from the sweeter frozen drinks out there. Adjust the simple syrup to your taste. If you're looking for a more classic paloma, an on-the-rocks variation can be found on page 85.

an on-the-rocks variation can be found on page 85.

MAKES 4–6
DRINKS

½ cup blanco tequila

1 grapefruit, juiced

1 lime, juiced

1–2 ounces simple syrup, to taste

4–6 cups ice

1 (12-ounce) can grapefruit hard seltzer

✦ Add everything but the seltzer to a blender, and blend until the desired slushy texture is reached.

✦ Add the seltzer and pulse a few times.

✦ Serve immediately.

the **HARD SELTZER** cocktail book

Magic Margarita (Frozen)

The ultimate frozen drink is the margarita. As with the frozen daiquiri recipe on page 66, hard seltzer is the magic ingredient here when it comes to flavors. Just swap out the lime seltzer for your favorite flavor. I suggest mango!

MAKES 4–6 DRINKS

1 lime wedge, for salt rim (optional)

sea salt, for salt rim (optional)

½ cup blanco tequila

2 ounces Cointreau

1 lime, juiced

1–2 ounces simple syrup, to taste

6–8 cups ice

1 (12-ounce) can lime hard seltzer

✦ If desired, rub the lime wedge around the rim of the serving glasses to moisten. Dip each rim in the sea salt to coat.

✦ Add all the ingredients except the seltzer to a blender. Blend until smooth.

✦ Add the seltzer. Pulse a few times until just combined.

✦ Serve in the prepared glasses.

Feelin' Bubbly Aperol Raspberry Float

This combines so many delicious things: Aperol, ice cream, hard seltzer, and even fresh fruit (look, it's healthy!). Great as a dessert cocktail—but honestly, don't be held back by time of day.

MAKES 4 DRINKS

1 cup fresh raspberries

4 ounces Aperol

2 cups vanilla or raspberry ice cream

2 (12-ounce) cans raspberry hard seltzer

✦ Divide the raspberries evenly among four large glasses. Add 1 ounce of Aperol to each glass. Muddle.

✦ Divide the ice cream evenly among the glasses (½ cup each). Top each glass with half a can (6 ounces) of seltzer.

✦ Serve immediately.

CHAPTER THREE

Classy Classics

I'm sure the traditionalists out there will call this section sacrilege, but sometimes we have to mix it up. They're classics for a reason, but surely we can *zhuzh* them up a bit!

Hard seltzer gets a bad rap sometimes, but it shouldn't be left out when it comes to a classy night in. There are so many cocktails out there that benefit from a few bubbles, and hard seltzer is the perfect addition if you want to punch up your favorites. And don't think that hard seltzer can only be mixed with clear liquor. You can still mix it up with the darker rums and whiskeys as long as you have the right flavors in mind.

Millennial Cosmo

We'd have to believe a millennial Carrie Bradshaw couldn't turn down the Claw—it's now a staple at NYC bars and rooftop parties. I couldn't help but wonder: what would the rest of the girls think of this seltzer-y variation?

MAKES 2 DRINKS

2 ounces vodka

2 ounces cranberry juice

1 ounce Cointreau or triple sec

1 (12-ounce) can lime hard seltzer

lime wedges or peel, for garnish (optional)

✦ Fill a cocktail shaker with ice. Add the vodka, cranberry juice, and Cointreau or triple sec to the shaker. Shake until chilled.

✦ Strain into two (ideally chilled) glasses.

✦ Top each glass with half a can (6 ounces) of seltzer. Garnish with the lime wedges or peel.

> If you want to go with the classic martini-shaped glass (aka a cocktail glass), make sure you've got oversized ones on hand. This seltzer variation will not fit in your cute Gatsby-esque coupes.

Poppin' Paloma

If you're running short on ingredients, you can just combine the tequila and the grapefruit seltzer and call it a day. But I recommend including the juices listed here. They make even the lower-shelf tequilas go down so much smoother!

MAKES 2 DRINKS

2 lime wedges, for salt rim and garnish (optional)

sea salt, for salt rim (optional)

4 ounces blanco tequila

4 ounces grapefruit juice

1 ounce lime juice

1 (12-ounce) can grapefruit hard seltzer

rosemary sprigs, for garnish (optional)

✦ If a salt rim is desired, rub a lime wedge around the rims of two glasses to moisten. Dip the rim of each glass in the sea salt.

✦ Fill the two glasses with ice. Add the tequila, grapefruit juice, and lime juice. Stir briefly.

✦ Top each glass with half a can (6 ounces) of seltzer. Garnish with a lime wedge and/or rosemary sprig for added class.

Summer in Moscow Mule

Attention, comrades! Summer in Moscow is here with this spiked seltzer variation on the classic Moscow mule. Ginger beer is an absolute must for this recipe; feel free to add more if desired.

MAKES 4 DRINKS

4 ounces vodka

1 (12-ounce) can lime hard seltzer

1 (12-ounce) bottle ginger beer

fresh mint, for garnish

lime wheels, for garnish

✦ Fill four copper mugs with ice. Add 1 ounce of the vodka to each glass.

✦ Split the seltzer and the ginger beer among the four mugs.

✦ Stir and garnish with the fresh mint and lime wheels.

Midsummer Mojito

I don't always love a lime hard seltzer (sometimes it's just a little boring). The mojito is the perfect way to jazz it up. Fresh mint is a must-have!

MAKES 2 DRINKS

10 mint leaves

1 ounce simple syrup

4 ounces white rum

2 ounces lime juice

1 (12-ounce) can lime hard seltzer

✦ Split the mint leaves and the simple syrup between two glasses. Muddle.

✦ Split the rum and the lime juice between the glasses. Stir.

✦ Fill the glasses with ice. Top off each with half a can (6 ounces) of seltzer.

Fizzier French 75

Mixing sparkling white wine with hard seltzer doubles the bubbles when compared to the classic French 75. Use wine glasses instead of the traditional champagne flute, because you'll need extra room for all the bubbles in this recipe!

MAKES 2 DRINKS

3 ounces gin

1 ounce lemon juice

1 ounce simple syrup (optional)

4 ounces prosecco or other sparkling white wine

1 (12-ounce) can lemon hard seltzer

lemon twists, for garnish

✦ Fill a cocktail shaker with ice. Add the gin, lemon juice, and simple syrup, if using. Shake until very cold.

✦ Fill two wine glasses with ice. Strain the mixture into the glasses.

✦ Top each glass with 2 ounces of prosecco and half a can (6 ounces) of seltzer. Stir briefly. Garnish each with a lemon twist.

The optional simple syrup is for those who like a little extra sweetness.

Twisted Martini

While James Bond certainly wouldn't order this bastardization of a martini, we had to give this cinematic classic a bubbly twist.

MAKES 2 DRINKS

¼ cup gin

1 ounce dry vermouth

1 can (12-ounce) lemon hard seltzer

lemon twists (optional)

✦ Fill a cocktail shaker with ice, and add the gin and vermouth.

✦ Stir! Don't shake.

✦ Strain into two (ideally chilled) glasses.

✦ Top each glass with half a can (6 ounces) of seltzer. Garnish with a lemon twists.

The more vermouth you add, the "wetter" a martini gets. If you like your martinis dry, rinse the interior of your glass with the dry vermouth instead of adding it to the shaker with the other ingredients.

Down-and-Dirty Martini

Mixing olive juice and hard seltzer is a delicate balancing act, but it can be done! Although a bit strange at first, it certainly starts to grow on you by the time you've reached the bottom of your glass. Or maybe that's just the alcohol?

MAKES 2 DRINKS

¼ cup gin

1 ounce dry vermouth

1 ounce olive juice (optional)

1 (12-ounce) can lemon hard seltzer

olives, for garnish

✦ Fill a cocktail shaker with ice. Add the gin, vermouth, and olive juice, if using.

✦ Stir! Don't shake.

✦ Strain into two (ideally chilled) glasses.

✦ Top each glass with half a can (6 ounces) of seltzer. Garnish each glass with 1 to 3 olives, to taste.

> James Bond was wrong—you should always stir instead of shake when it comes to martinis. Shaking actually breaks off little pieces of ice that water down your drink.

Classy AF Gin Fizz

Do not be afraid of egg whites! The egg whites make this cocktail classy AF. You will be sure to impress when you shake up these extra-fizzy gin fizzes. I do not recommend skimping on the simple syrup and lemon juice here. All are necessary for a proper fizz; the lemon seltzer just brings it all together.

MAKES 2 DRINKS

¼ cup gin

2 ounces lemon juice

1 ounce simple syrup

2 egg whites

1 (12-ounce) can lemon hard seltzer

lemon wedges or peel, for garnish (optional)

✦ Fill a cocktail shaker with ice. Pour the gin, lemon juice, simple syrup, and egg whites into the shaker. Really shake this one up.

✦ Strain into two tall glasses.

✦ Top each glass with half a can (6 ounces) of seltzer. Garnish with the lemon wedges or peel.

Gimme More Gimlet

A gimlet is simple, classic, and timeless. Lime hard seltzer is required here; using any other flavor would result in an entirely different drink!

MAKES 2 DRINKS

¼ cup gin

1 ounce lime juice

1 ounce simple syrup

1 (12-ounce) can lime hard seltzer

✦ Fill a cocktail shaker with ice. Add the gin, lime juice, and simple syrup. Shake until well chilled.

✦ Strain into two glasses.

✦ Top each glass with half a can (6 ounces) of seltzer.

Claw Collins

There is literally no better cocktail for hard seltzer than the Tom Collins. Just swap out the club soda, and you've got your very own "Claw Collins."

MAKES 2 DRINKS

4 ounces gin

2 ounces lemon juice

1 ounce simple syrup

1 (12-ounce) can lemon hard seltzer

lemon wedges, for garnish (optional)

maraschino cherries, for garnish (optional)

✦ Fill two glasses with ice. Split the gin, lemon juice, and simple syrup between the glasses.

✦ Top each glass with half a can (6 ounces) of seltzer. Stir.

✦ Garnish each glass with a lemon wedge and a maraschino cherry, if desired.

National Treasure Negroni

This recipe is inspired by National Treasure Stanley Tucci. The "Tooch" went viral in the spring of 2020 after releasing a delightful video detailing his extra-boozy Negroni recipe. This adaption has that same spirit (and a lot of spirits). Enjoy carefully, and may the odds be ever in your favor.

MAKES 2 DRINKS

¼ cup gin

2 ounces sweet vermouth

2 ounces Campari

1 (12-ounce) can orange hard seltzer

2 orange slices, for garnish (optional)

✦ Fill a cocktail shaker with ice. Pour the gin, vermouth, and Campari into the shaker. Really shake this one up.

✦ Strain into two ice-filled double old-fashioned glasses.

✦ Top each glass with half a can (6 ounces) of seltzer. Garnish each with an orange slice.

New Old Fashioned

We'll give this iconic *Mad Men* cocktail a modern spin by adding a few ounces of orange hard seltzer into the mix. We know that Don Draper would not be a hard seltzer guy, but with that bone structure we certainly won't hold it against him.

MAKES 1 DRINK

1 sugar cube

1 dash bitters (like Angostura)

1 teaspoon water

1 ounce bourbon

½ (12-ounce) can orange hard seltzer (approximately 6 ounces)

orange peel, for garnish

maraschino cherry, for garnish

✦ Put the sugar cube, dash of bitters, and water in a double old-fashioned glass. Muddle.

✦ Add the bourbon and the seltzer. Stir gently.

✦ Garnish with the orange peel and maraschino cherry.

> If you don't have sugar cubes on hand, here's a hint: 1 sugar cube = 1 teaspoon sugar.

Everyday Boulevardier

The *New York Times* recently declared the boulevardier the "perfect" Thanksgiving cocktail, so we had to try a spin on it. You can certainly enjoy this all year round, but it's especially great when you're trying to avoid conversation with awkward cousins and opinionated uncles.

MAKES 2 DRINKS

2 ounces rye or bourbon

1 ounce Campari

1 ounce sweet vermouth

1 (12-ounce) can orange hard seltzer

orange peel, for garnish

✦ Fill a cocktail shaker with ice. Add the rye or bourbon, Campari, and vermouth. Stir.

✦ Fill two glasses with ice. Strain the mixture into the prepared glasses.

✦ Top each glass with half a can (6 ounces) of seltzer. Garnish with orange peel.

Southern Seltzer Mint Julep

What is more refreshing than spiked seltzer on hot and humid Derby Day? Next time you have guests, show them some proper Southern hospitality and mix up this winning combination.

MAKES 2 DRINKS

10 fresh mint leaves, plus 2 mint sprigs, for garnish

1 ounce simple syrup

4 ounces bourbon

1 (12-ounce) can lime hard seltzer

ice, crushed

✦ Rinse and dry the mint. Split the mint between two glasses, reserving the two sprigs for a garnish.

✦ Put ½ ounce of the simple syrup in each glass. Muddle the mint and the syrup.

✦ Split the bourbon and the seltzer between the two glasses.

✦ Top each glass with crushed ice and garnish with a mint sprig.

Summer in the City Manhattan

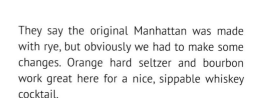

They say the original Manhattan was made with rye, but obviously we had to make some changes. Orange hard seltzer and bourbon work great here for a nice, sippable whiskey cocktail.

MAKES 2 DRINKS

¼ cup bourbon

1 ounce sweet vermouth

2 dashes bitters (like Angostura)

1 (12-ounce) can orange hard seltzer

maraschino cherries, for garnish

✦ Fill a cocktail shaker with ice. Add the bourbon, vermouth, bitters, and hard seltzer. Mix.

✦ Strain into two glasses. Garnish each with a maraschino cherry.

Snap, Sparkle, Sazerac

Bring a little bit of New Orleans to any party with this twist on one of the city's many iconic cocktails.

MAKES 2 DRINKS

2 sugar cubes

6 dashes bitters (like Peychaud's)

2 teaspoons water

3 ounces rye

1 (12-ounce) can lemon hard seltzer

+ Chill two double old-fashioned glasses.

+ In a cocktail shaker, combine the sugar cubes, bitters, and water. Muddle.

+ Add the rye and seltzer. Stir.

+ Strain into the chilled glasses.

(CHAPTER FOUR)

Pregame & Party

While the bubbly concoctions offered in the previous chapters are certainly boozy, they all try to find the balance between buzzed and blackout. In this chapter, I've thrown that out the window. This is the real party.

Ranging from classy to absolutely trashy, this chapter has everything from Holiday Party Punch and Cucumber Lime Coolers to Jell-O shots and jungle juice. Make sure you've got a lot of ice and a large punch bowl on hand.

Enter at your own risk, and be sure to hydrate.

Truly LIIT (Long Island Iced Tea)

I know it. You know it. No explanation necessary. I've scaled it back the tiniest bit to account for average glass sizes, but feel free to increase the liquor amounts as desired. You only live once.

MAKES 2 DRINKS

½ ounce vodka

½ ounce rum

½ ounce tequila

½ ounce gin

2–4 ounces cola, to taste

1 (12-ounce) can black cherry or lemon hard seltzer

lime wedges, for garnish

✦ Fill a cocktail shaker with ice. Add the vodka, rum, tequila, and gin. Shake.

✦ Strain into two glasses filled with ice.

✦ Top each glass with 1–2 ounces of cola and half a can (6 ounces) of seltzer. Garnish each with a lime wedge.

There are few recipes where I recommend black cherry hard seltzer. It's for a good reason: black cherry is an extremely overpowering flavor, and you won't get to taste anything else in your cocktail. But in this case...maybe that's for the best?

Adios Mother Fizzer

The "AMF" is not too different from the Truly LIIT...except this one is blue. Be warned: despite its playful color, this drink is not playing. It is 100 percent booze.

MAKES 2 DRINKS

½ ounce vodka

½ ounce rum

½ ounce tequila

½ ounce gin

1 ounce blue curaçao

1 (12-ounce) can orange hard seltzer

✦ Fill a cocktail shaker with ice, and add all the ingredients but the seltzer. Shake until well chilled.

✦ Strain into two glasses filled with ice. Top each with half a can (6 ounces) of seltzer.

Sparkling Jell-O Shots

No party is complete without Jell-O shots! Make these at least 4 hours ahead so that they are completely set by the time your party is in full swing.

APPROXIMATELY 15 SHOTS

1 (3-ounce) package strawberry Jell-O gelatin

1 cup water, boiling

½ cup lime hard seltzer, chilled

½ cup vodka, chilled

✦ In a large glass measuring cup or mixing bowl, combine the gelatin and the boiling water. Stir until the gelatin is completely dissolved.

✦ Add the seltzer and the vodka. Stir well.

✦ Pour the Jell-O mixture into plastic condiment cups. Cover and allow to set for at least 4 hours in the fridge.

Rum One-Two-Three Punch

This party pleaser will pack a punch with not one, not two, but three types of alcohol. Feel free to sub in other citrus or tropical flavors here if you don't have pineapple seltzer handy.

MAKES 4-6 DRINKS

½ cup light rum

½ cup dark rum

¼ cup lime juice

1 cup orange juice

1 ounce grenadine

2 (12-ounce) cans pineapple hard seltzer

ice, as needed

limes, sliced, for garnish

pineapple wedges (roughly ½-inch thick), for garnish

+ In a punch bowl or large pitcher, combine all the ingredients except the lime slices and pineapple wedges.

+ Float the lime slices. Garnish glasses with pineapple wedges by cutting a small slit in each wedge and placing it on the rim of the glass.

Lemon Drop It Like It's Hot

A sweetened-up version of the martini, the lemon drop is always a crowd pleaser. Heavy on gin and hard seltzer, it packs a greater punch than you think.

MAKES 2 DRINKS

¼ cup gin

1 ounce simple syrup

1 ounce lemon juice

1 (12-ounce) can lemon hard seltzer

2 lemon wedges, for garnish

sugar rim, for garnish (optional)

✦ Fill a cocktail shaker with ice. Add the gin, simple syrup, and lemon juice. Shake until chilled.

✦ If a sugar rim is desired, rub a lemon wedge around the rims of two over-sized cocktail glasses to moisten. Dip the rims in sugar to coat.

✦ Strain the chilled mixture into the prepared glasses. Top each glass with half a can (6 ounces) of seltzer. Garnish each with a lemon wedge.

Seltz on the Beach

Opt for this cocktail instead of sex on the beach. (I mean, think about it. Sand. Everywhere.) This is a bachelorette party classic when combined with any bridesmaid's best friend: spiked seltzer.

MAKES 4 DRINKS

1 cup vodka

½ cup peach schnapps

1 cup orange juice

1 cup cranberry juice

1 (12-ounce) can grapefruit hard seltzer

orange slices, for garnish

maraschino cherries, for garnish

✦ Combine all the ingredients except the garnishes in a pitcher.

✦ Serve over ice. Garnish each glass with an orange slice and a maraschino cherry.

Mermaid Punch

I can't promise Ariel-quality hair, but I can help you live your best mermaid life with this delicious aquamarine punch. Surely King Trident would disapprove, but what can you do? You wanna be where the people are.

MAKES 6–8 DRINKS

½ cup blue curaçao

1 cup light rum

1 cup pineapple juice

1 (750-milliliter) bottle prosecco or other sparkling white wine

2 (12-ounce) cans pineapple hard seltzer

pineapple wedges (roughly ½-inch thick), for garnish

maraschino cherries, for garnish

✦ Fill a large pitcher or punch bowl with ice. Pour in the curaçao, rum, and pineapple juice.

✦ If making ahead, refrigerate at this stage until ready to serve.

✦ Just before serving, top with the prosecco and the hard seltzer. Garnish individual glasses with pineapple and cherries, if desired. Serve immediately.

Any tropical-flavor hard seltzer will work here. Pineapple is the most on-theme, but the citrus flavors also work well.

Apple-Picking Punch

Every time I go apple picking, I end up with approximately 50 apples and a bunch of cider. This is a great way to make a dent in your peck.

MAKES 8–12 DRINKS

CINNAMON SUGAR RIM
½ cup sugar

1 tablespoon ground cinnamon

1 orange slice

PUNCH
1 cup bourbon

½ gallon apple cider or juice, chilled

4 apples, sliced

2 oranges, sliced

6 cinnamon sticks

2 (12-ounce) cans hard seltzer, in a seasonal flavor like Bud Light's Apple Crisp

ice, as needed

✦ To make the cinnamon sugar rim, combine sugar and cinnamon in a small bowl. Rub an orange slice around the rims of 6–8 glasses to moisten. Dip the rims in the cinnamon sugar to coat.

✦ In a large punch bowl, combine all the punch ingredients.

✦ Place the prepared glasses near the punch bowl and allow guests to serve themselves!

I realize not all seasonal seltzers may be available to you, so use your best judgment here. Many cideries have also come out with hard seltzers that would work great!

Holiday Party Punch

Ring in the holidays with this festively themed red sangria. And don't forget, a case of hard seltzer (along with this book) makes a great holiday gift!

MAKES 6–8 DRINKS

1 bottle dry red wine

½ cup brandy or cognac

2–4 ounces simple syrup, to taste

1 green apple, sliced

1 orange, sliced

½ cup fresh cranberries

2 (12-ounce) cans orange, raspberry, or seasonal-flavor hard seltzer

ice, as needed

rosemary sprigs, for garnish

✦ In a large pitcher or punch bowl, combine all the ingredients except the rosemary.

✦ If making ahead, combine all the ingredients except the seltzer, ice, and rosemary. Refrigerate. When ready to serve, add the seltzer and the ice, and stir. Allow guests to serve themselves and garnish with rosemary, if desired.

the **HARD SELTZER** *cocktail book*

Lost in the Jungle Juice

No explanation needed. Get a large beverage dispenser (at least 4 gallons) or an empty cooler, and, of course, feel free to improvise. Good luck and Godspeed.

MAKES 30 DRINKS

12 (12-ounce) cans citrus-flavor hard seltzer

1 (750-milliliter) bottle vodka

1 gallon lemonade

½ gallon orange juice

½ gallon fruit punch

3 oranges, sliced

ice, as needed

✦ In a very large bowl, pitcher, or beverage cooler, combine all the ingredients but the ice.

✦ Stir. Fill with ice.

> You can get a pack of just one flavor or a variety pack of citrus flavors. The tropical variety pack would also work well here!

Sweet Tea for a Crowd

This is not your grandma's sweet tea. A little boost from hard seltzer makes this a sparkling and sweet summer treat. Adjust simple syrup to taste; if you're a true Southerner, use the full amount.

MAKES 6–8 DRINKS

12 tea bags black tea

4 cups boiling water

ice, as needed

¾–1 cup simple syrup, to taste

1 cup bourbon

2 (12-ounce) cans lemon hard seltzer

lemon wedges, for garnish

fresh mint, for garnish

✦ Combine the tea bags and boiling water. Allow to steep for 5 minutes. Remove the tea bags.

✦ Fill a pitcher with ice. Pour in the tea.

✦ Add the simple syrup, bourbon, and seltzer. If making ahead, wait to add the seltzer until ready to serve. Stir.

✦ Serve with additional ice and lemon wedges, and garnish with mint.

Cucumber Lime Cooler

Simple and refreshing, this is a great last-minute cocktail for a hot day. Just throw everything in 5 minutes before people show up, and you'll look like you totally have your shit together.

MAKES 6–8 DRINKS

10–15 fresh mint leaves

2–3 ounces simple syrup, to taste

1 cup gin

2 (12-ounce) cans lime hard seltzer

2 cucumbers, sliced

1 lime, sliced

1 lemon, sliced

ice, as needed

+ Add the mint and the simple syrup to a pitcher. Muddle.

+ Add the remaining ingredients. Stir.

+ Serve over additional ice.

Recipe Index

Acknowledgments

Thanks to the entire team at Ulysses Press, who have supported me and all of my craziest ideas for many years. They've seen my highs and my lows (particularly at boozy brunch). Major thanks to Anne Healey, Renee Rutledge, Jake Flaherty, and Production Queen Claire Chun for pulling this together into an actual book.

The fabulous cover of this book was designed by the equally fabulous David Hastings, who I put through the ringer to get this one right.

I have to thank my dear friends who make up the Haus of Eleganza in Brooklyn. They've taught me everything I know about day drinking.

Lastly, I have to thank my dear Michael Calcagno, who enthusiastically drank a lot of seltzer. In cold weather. During a pandemic. Where you ride, I ride.

About the Author

Casie Vogel is a lover of all things carbonated, whether it's a hard seltzer or a Diet Coke. She has experience both hosting and attending many a boozy brunch that has transitioned into an all-night affair, thanks to well-mixed drinks. She lives in Brooklyn.